⊕ur Catholic Life

A READING AND STUDY GUIDE FOR ADULT FAITH FORMATION

2

+ CREED +

THE
MYSTERY
OF GOD

Bill Huebsch

TWENTY-THIRD PUBLICATIONS
twentythirdpublications.com

IMPRIMATUR

+ Most Reverend Joseph R. Binzer
Auxiliary Bishop
Archdiocese of Cincinnati
February 9, 2016

The *Imprimatur* ("Permission to
Publish") is a declaration that a
book or pamphlet is considered
to be free of doctrinal or moral
error. It is not implied that those
who have granted the *Imprimatur*
agree with the contents, opinions,
or statements expressed.

Scripture texts are from the *New Revised Standard Version Bible:
Catholic Edition*, copyright 1989, 1993, Division of Christian Education
of the National Council of the Churches of Christ in the United States
of America. Used by permission. All rights reserved.

Twenty-Third Publications
1 Montauk Avenue, Suite 200, New London, CT 06320
(860) 437-3012 » (800) 321-0411 » www.twentythirdpublications.com

ISBN: 978-1-62785-168-8
Library of Congress Catalog Card Number: 2016939656
Printed in the U.S.A.

Contents

How to use this study guide in six small-group sessions

Gather. As people arrive for each session, welcome them warmly and offer them refreshments. You may wish to have sacred music playing to set the tone. If people are new to each other, name tags can help break the ice. When everyone has arrived, gather your group and invite them to open their books to today's material.

Begin with *Lectio divina* prayer. Each session opens with a short and prayerful reflection on a scriptural text that is found in that section of the *Catechism*. Here are the steps:

1. Begin with the Sign of the Cross.

2. Read aloud the Introduction for this session.

3. Call everyone to prayer using these or similar words: *Let us turn our hearts to Christ now and hear the word of the Lord.*

4. Invite a member of the group to proclaim the Scripture we present for you.

5. Invite your group members to share about the text, first in twos and threes if you wish, and then as a whole group. Sharing: *What word or phrase in this reading catches your ear? What is God saying to us in this scriptural text?*

6. Now pray in these or similar words:
   O God, we know that you are with us and that you behold all we are about to do. Now grant that, by the power of the Holy Spirit, we might be faithful as we study our faith and charitable in how we treat each other. Through Christ, our Lord. Amen.

Read. Moving around the circle in your group and rotating readers, read aloud each numbered faith statement. Group members should note items in the material that strike them as especially important. Do not read aloud the **We Believe** statements. They are provided as an enhancement to the text.

Group or personal process. When you come to the process notes, pause to continue around the circle, discussing as the notes direct. Use our suggestions as a starting point, and add your own questions, prayers, or action plans.

Finish. As you conclude this session, call everyone to prayer once again. Reread the scriptural text we used in the beginning. Then move around the circle one last time to share: *In light of this reading and what we have learned today, what has touched you most deeply? What new insight of faith will you carry away from here? What new questions about faith have arisen for you? How will today's discussion work its way into your daily life?* Close your session with the prayer we provide, or lead a spontaneous prayer in which everyone shares their own prayer.

Session One

BASED ON ARTICLES 50–67 OF THE *CATECHISM OF THE CATHOLIC CHURCH*. TO READ A SUMMARY OF THIS SECTION, SEE *CATECHISM* ARTICLES 68–73

Introduction

As we turn to study the mystery of God, we begin with one large thought: out of love, God has revealed and given God's own self to us. God has acted toward us with a loving heart, and in doing so has revealed the divine to us by gradually communicating God's own mystery in deeds and in words. We are studying mystery here, so we cannot treat it like science; these are *faith statements*. But we believe that God has communicated God's own self to us from the beginning of the human race, a powerful and life-changing understanding of the actions of God. And even more, we believe that God has revealed God's own self most fully through Jesus Christ, through whom God has established an eternal covenant with our human family.

Scripture

READER: A reading from the Letter to the Ephesians.

With all wisdom and insight he has made known to us the mystery of his will, according to his good pleasure that he set forth in Christ, as a plan for the fullness of time, to gather up all things in him, things in heaven and things on earth. In Christ we have also obtained an inheritance, having been destined according to the purpose of him who accomplishes all things according to his counsel and will, so that we, who were the first to set our hope on Christ, might live for the praise of his glory. In him you also, when you had heard the word of truth, the gospel of your salvation, and had believed in him, were marked with the seal of the promised Holy Spirit.

(EPHESIANS 1:8–13)

READER: The word of the Lord.

ALL: Thanks be to God.

PART ONE + ARTICLES 50–54 OF THE *CATECHISM*
Where do we meet God?

[1] "God is love," we read in 1 John 4:8. One cannot really *see* love with human eyes or *hear it* with the human ear. Yet using our own powers of observation, reason, and sound thinking, we can come to know God.

[2] We can be certain of the presence of God because we can see the powerful outcomes which are "the works" that God has done. These works begin with the creation of the entire world including us humans and are followed by a continual journey through history as God touched the human family again and again with his love.

[3] But we can also come to know God because God has chosen to freely, generously, and lovingly reveal the divine heart to us. God has, in a word, given us a glimpse of mystery which is the divine plan of loving goodness formed and carried out down through history.

[4] This divine plan culminated in Christ, who is love revealed in all its marvelous fullness. Through Christ all we need to know about God was fully revealed. The *Constitution on Divine Revelation* from Vatican II tells us about this. "It pleased God, in his goodness and wisdom," the Constitution says in article 2, "to reveal himself and to make known the mystery of his will, which was that people can draw near to the Father, through Christ, the Word made flesh, in the Holy Spirit, and thus become sharers in the divine nature."

WE BELIEVE

God has revealed himself to us as love. He has given himself to us humans. In this way, God provides us with answers to the deep questions about meaning and purpose that we all ponder.

[5] By his very nature God is communicative. God wants to communicate the divine life to us because we are the people he freely created. This makes us all sons and daughters of God! God wants us to be able to respond to the divine voice, to know God's own heart, and to love far beyond our natural capacity.

[6] The *Constitution on Divine Revelation* goes on in article 2: "The pattern of [God's revelation to us] unfolds through deeds and words...the deeds...confirm the doctrine and realities signified by the words...and the words, for their part, proclaim the deeds and bring to light the mystery they contain."

[7] In this way, God slowly communicates God's own self to us, preparing us by stages to accept divine revelation. This revelation has come down through history and culminates in Jesus Christ.

[8] God showed from the beginning of human life what the divine

heart was like: a heart full of love. God invited us to intimacy and placed within us the seeds of divine life: grace, love, justice, and goodness.

[9] When we failed to love God in return, this desire to show the divine heart to us humans did not wane. God remained with us and did not stop loving us.

Group or personal process

- When those closest to you "reveal" themselves, how do they do it?

- How do you reveal yourself to others? Name both the words and the actions you might use to show someone else who you really are.

- How do you "meet God" as you observe the words and deeds he has done? Read faith statements #5 and #6 again as you respond to this question.

- Think about all of creation, the people around you, and the teachings passed on from generation to generation about forgiveness, mercy, and love. What have you come to know about God through all these signs?

The promise

[10] In fact, God kept promising salvation, redemption, and eternal life. Down through history this desire to be close to us has never ceased.

[11] Recall the words of our own Eucharistic Prayer at Mass: "And when through disobedience [we] had lost your friendship, you did not abandon [us] to the domain of death....Time and again you offered [us] covenants..."

The covenant with Noah

[12] Sin became a reality in the human race, but God stayed with us through it all. Scripture speaks of the covenant with Noah after the flood. It describes how God responds to us. The Book of Genesis is where you find this story. In chapter 9, verses 8–13, God speaks to Noah and to us:

[14] "As for me, I am establishing my covenant with you and your descendants after you and with every living creature that is with you, the birds, the domestic animals, and every animal of the earth with you...I establish my covenant with you...this is the sign: I have set my bow in the clouds and it shall be a sign..."

[15] Without this covenant with God, we humans have no hope of living together in peace. Without this closeness with God, sin would overtake the world. Without this close covenant, in short, the human race would be lost!

God chooses Abraham

[16] Reading further in the Book of Genesis, chapter 12 beginning with verse 1, we find the next chapter in the divine story: God then called Abram from his country, his family, and his father's house.

[17] God named him Abraham, a name that means "father of many nations." "In you," God said to Abraham and Sarah, "all the families of the earth shall be blessed." The people descended from Sarah and Abraham became the ancestors of the Church that we know.

WE BELIEVE
The covenant God made with all creatures
and with the human family will last forever.

---

[18] God continued to gradually gather his people into a family, and we continue to honor them all: patriarchs, prophets, and other Old Testament figures.

God forms the people of Israel

[19] The great works of God were far from over. God formed Israel as God's own people by freeing them from slavery in Egypt.

[20] At Mount Sinai, God established the covenant with them and gave them the law through Moses. The law would help them remain faithful to God as the one living and true God, the Father, the judge, and eventually, the Savior.

[21] As the *Constitution on Divine Revelation* puts it in article 3, "throughout the ages, [God] prepared the way for the Gospel." The people of Israel were the first to hear the word of God. The prophets later delivered God's message more forcefully, and the wonderful

message was that this people should hope for salvation, a new and lasting covenant intended for all and written on their very hearts. The prophets proclaimed that God offers salvation for all, forgiveness from their sins, and hope for eternal life.

WE BELIEVE

The covenant with Abraham and his descendants is the basis on which God formed his people. Through Moses, God revealed the law to them.

---

[22] This message was often carried by the poor, as the *Catechism* reminds us in article 64, and by holy women such as Sarah, Rebecca, Rachel, Miriam, Deborah, Hannah, Judith, and Esther. And when the time was right, God continued to reach out to us through Mary, who became the mother of Jesus.

Group or personal process

- What part of this story of God's saving actions in history speaks most loudly to your heart and soul?

- Who has told this story of salvation to you? Which men or women in your life have revealed God to you?

- How do you respond to faith statement #22? How have the poor and powerless revealed God to you?

God's Word

[23] "In the beginning was the Word," John's gospel tells us in chapter 1, verse 1, "and the Word was with God, and the Word was God."

[24] "Long ago," the Letter to the Hebrews says in chapter 1, verses 1 and 2, "God spoke to our ancestors in many and various ways by the prophets, but in these last days he has spoken to us by a Son..."

[25] God spoke one amazing, perfect, and complete Word to us and that Word is Jesus Christ the Son of God, now human. We await no further Word.

WE BELIEVE

God has revealed himself fully to us through Jesus Christ, his Son. The covenant established through Jesus is eternal. We expect no further revelation.

[26] If we focus our attentions on Christ and fix our gaze upon his Cross, we will come to understand all that God spoke through prophets, patriarchs, or first parents. Here God reveals all he wishes to tell us about love, forgiveness, generosity, and God's own Spirit.

[27] And yet, even though revelation is complete in Christ, not everything that the gospel demands of us here in our time, here in this age, has yet been fully revealed. Or if it has been revealed, then it has not been fully understood by us. Christians must be alert and steadfast as down through the centuries we gradually grasp the full significance of the gospel.

[28] Certain private revelations have occurred, and some of them have been recognized by the Church community through its leaders. They are meant to strengthen faith and help us cope in certain moments of history, but they do not add to Christ.

[29] For us Catholics, no revelation that surpasses that of Christ is expected. Indeed, we people of faith gather as God's family and community. We are the Church, and we are huddled together with the hope of ever greater love, justice, and peace. Our hope is rooted in Christ, who has given us the power of God.

[30] God's communication of the divine heart to us is nothing less than grace itself. Our response to God's free, generous, and loving gift of grace is faith. We believe; this means we adopt the way of life that fulfills our destiny as children of God. We desire to become loving, forgiving, without judgment, and full of mercy.

[31] On this we can rely: God is known to us because God has given his own self to us with love. For, as chapter 1 of the *Constitution on Divine Revelation* says in its conclusion, "those things, which in themselves are not beyond the grasp of human reason, can, in the present condition of the human race, be known by all with ease, with firm certainty, and without the contamination of error."

Group or personal process

- As you think about it, what have we humans not yet fully understood about what God wants for us? Read faith statement #27 again as you reflect on this.

- How have we failed to live up to our destiny as children of God? What would you suggest we do to become more faithful?

Prayer

Father, throughout the ages you have offered us a relationship with you. Even when we remained selfish, when we failed to live with the self-giving love which you have implanted in our hearts, you reached out to offer us a covenant. We now turn our hearts back to you once again, ready and willing to be your sons and daughters. We open ourselves to your love and forgiveness. Strengthen us and increase our faith. We pray through Christ, our Lord. Amen.

Session Two

BASED ON ARTICLES 101–133 OF THE *CATECHISM OF THE CATHOLIC CHURCH*. TO READ A SUMMARY OF THIS SECTION, SEE *CATECHISM* ARTICLES 134–141

Introduction

We have just considered God's loving plan for us, demonstrated in powerful words and deeds throughout history. Now we turn our attention to sacred Scripture. We believe that God is the author of sacred Scripture because God inspired its human authors to write what they did. The interpretation of Scripture must be attentive above all to what God wants to reveal through the writing done by these sacred authors. We seek to understand God's word in the texts over which we read and pray. The Church accepts and venerates as inspired the 46 books of the Old Testament and the 27 books of the New Testament. We honor them all and treat them all as sacred; but the four gospels occupy a central place for us Christians because Christ Jesus is their center.

Scripture

READER: A reading from the Gospel of Luke.

Since many have undertaken to set down an orderly account of the events that have been fulfilled among us, just as they were handed on to us by those who from the beginning were eyewitnesses and servants of the word, I too decided, after investigating everything carefully from the very first, to write an orderly account for you, most excellent Theophilus, so that you may know the truth concerning the things about which you have been instructed. (LUKE 1:1-4)

READER: The word of the Lord.

ALL: Thanks be to God.

PART ONE + ARTICLES 101-108 OF THE *CATECHISM*
God's Word

[1] God has chosen to speak to us in our own language and God did this because it's in his nature to love us. Even more! God *is love.* Indeed, love is the very core of God's being, and sacred Scripture is the story of God loving us from the beginning right up to this present moment.

[2] There is great mystery in this: The Word of God became human, and human words are used to express the realities of God. In all the various books of the Bible, in all the various words used in Scripture, God speaks only one single Word: Jesus Christ. And in Jesus Christ, God expresses all there is to say!

[3] The Church has always venerated sacred Scripture in much the same way that the Church venerates the Body of Christ. Just as the Church continues throughout all time and in every place to celebrate the Eucharist and make present the Body of Christ, so the Church also celebrates the word.

[4] In sacred Scripture, in fact, we who are the Church constantly find our nourishment, our strength, and our road map for the journey of faith. The *Constitution on Divine Revelation* from Vatican II has a lovely way to describe all this. "In the sacred books," it says in article 21, "the Father who is in heaven comes lovingly to meet his children and talks with them."

WE BELIEVE

*The Scriptures contain the Word of God
and they are truly the inspired word of God.*

God as author

[5] We believe that God is the author of sacred Scripture. Turning once again to that beloved *Constitution on Divine Revelation*, to the opening line of chapter 3, we have a great summary of our beliefs. "Those things revealed by God," it says, "which are contained and presented in the text of Sacred Scripture have been written under the inspiration of the Holy Spirit."

[6] We Christians have a long history on which we build our faith. Our ancestors in the Church, from the most ancient times, believed that the hand of God was present and active in certain letters, stories, and collections of stories. Theirs was the first faith, and their early faith has become our own.

[7] Like them, therefore, we accept as sacred the collection of books that has come to be known as the Old and New Testaments. Certain human writers, we believe, were called to write sacred Scripture. God gave them the awesome vocation of using their own talents and abilities, in their own time and place, but God acted through them so that what they wrote is what God desired and no more.

[8] And because of God's hand in this, because of the role of the Spirit in this, we believe that Scripture teaches us clearly, faithfully, and truthfully only what God wants taught.

WE BELIEVE

God is the author of Scripture. He inspired the writers and acts through them to communicate with us. Thus, the words of Scripture are without error.

---

[9] The words of Scripture are not dead, because Christ lives among us! Christ is raised from the dead and it is the risen Lord to whom Scripture introduces us. It is Christ who helps us understand what we read.

Group or personal process

- When you have some quiet time for reflection and prayer, which words of Scripture come automatically to mind for you?

- What do you first remember about the Bible? How was the Bible used or not used in your family home?

- When did you first receive your own copy?

- Who helped you encounter Scripture?

The Spirit as teacher

[[10] In order for us to understand Scripture, we must understand that God is the author of sacred Scripture inasmuch as God intended and inspired what the authors affirmed by their words.

[11] The literal meaning of the words we read in the Bible is important to us, but we balance it by also understanding the intent of the authors, the audience to which they wrote, and the conditions of life that existed when the texts were first read.

[12] Because God chose human partners to write the text of Scripture, we must take into account where these authors lived, what their culture was like, and what was happening during their particular moment in history.

[13] What sort of literary devices did they use? Were they writing poetry or prose? Were they engaged in expressing prophetic texts or calling the people of their day to conversion? Were they writing narrative accounts of history? Whatever is the case, God speaks to us humans in these words.

WE BELIEVE
We interpret Scripture only with the guidance and power of the Holy Spirit. We cannot understand the texts without the help of the Spirit.

[14] Since the Bible is inspired, we must also read it in the light of the Holy Spirit. We should read Scripture as a whole, not citing this line or that to prove a particular point that we wish to believe. Scripture has an inherent unity, and no single line represents it all.

[15] We should always read Scripture taking into account the scholarship, research, and commentary that the Church provides for us. Scripture should not be interpreted privately but communally. Scripture lives in the very heart of the Church, after all. It is *lived by us*.

[16] We should read Scripture with faith in our own hearts, seeing within it what God desires for us. We look to the texts of sacred Scripture with two sets of eyes. We look first to see what the words themselves convey, opened up by scholars and interpreted together as a community. And we also look to see the meaning of these words beyond the merely literal. We look for the *spiritual realities* they communicate.

[17] We find in these texts stories that help us see greater realities and that give us a sign of divine life. So, for example, we read about the crossing of the Red Sea as the Hebrews left Egypt, and we see in this a sign of our own crossing over in baptism to new life in Christ. Or we might find in these texts examples and events that teach us how to live as God wants. Or we might find in these texts a way to understand spiritual realities that we have no way to describe: signs of eternal life.

[18] Those scholars who study Scripture should always do so to lead people to faith under the guidance of the whole Church, the whole community of God. Indeed, to the Church, the People of God, is entrusted the task of understanding, preserving, and guarding sacred Scripture.

Group or personal process

- What do you believe God wants to communicate to us through the words of sacred Scripture?

- How easy or difficult has it been for you to read and study Scripture? Talk together about the role of Scripture in your lives.

- How does the teaching in faith statements #16 and #17 help you understand Scripture and its purpose?

- Why do we avoid reading the texts of Scripture "literally" but instead read them with an ear to understanding their deeper original meaning?

PART THREE + ARTICLES 120–133 OF THE *CATECHISM*

The books of the Bible

[19] As we said above, it was through the faith of our early ancestors that we discerned which writings would be included in the Bible. We call this list "the canon of Scripture." The Bible includes 46 books in the Old Testament and 27 in the New Testament.

[20] The Old Testament includes the books of Genesis, Exodus, Leviticus, Numbers, and Deuteronomy, which form the Pentateuch or Torah.

[21] It includes the history and narrative books: Joshua, Judges, Ruth, 1 and 2 Samuel, 1 and 2 Kings, 1 and 2 Chronicles, Ezra and Nehemiah, Tobit, Judith, Esther, 1 and 2 Maccabees.

[22] It includes wisdom literature: Job, Psalms, Proverbs, Ecclesiastes, the Song of Songs, the Wisdom of Solomon, Sirach (Ecclesiasticus).

[23] And it includes the prophets: Isaiah, Jeremiah, Lamentations, Baruch, Ezekiel, Daniel, Hosea, Joel, Amos, Obadiah, Jonah, Micah,

Nahum, Habakkuk, Zephaniah, Haggai, Zachariah, and Malachi.

[24] The New Testament includes, of course, the four gospels of Matthew, Mark, Luke, and John, plus the Acts of the Apostles.

[25] It includes the letters of St. Paul to the Romans, 1 and 2 Corinthians, Galatians, Ephesians, Philippians, Colossians, 1 Thessalonians, and Philemon.

[26] It includes letters by Paul's followers and other leaders, including 2 Thessalonians, 1 and 2 Timothy, and Titus, the Letter to the Hebrews, the letters of James, 1 and 2 Peter, 1, 2, and 3 John, and Jude, and Revelation (the Apocalypse).

The Old Testament

[27] We Christians treat the Old Testament with great reverence. Even though we believe in Jesus Christ, we know that God's plan for us is told throughout the Old Testament and we really cannot fully understand the story of Christ unless we understand its background.

[28] Indeed, the writings of the Old Testament, according to the *Constitution on Divine Revelation*, "are a storehouse of sublime teaching on God and of sound wisdom on human life as well as a wonderful treasury of prayers; in them, too, the mystery of our salvation is implicitly present" (article 15).

[29] In short, we Christians venerate the Old Testament.

The New Testament

[30] We find the word of God, of course, to be profoundly expressed in the books of the New Testament. Here Jesus Christ is the central figure; he is God made flesh who is the light of the world. For us

Christians the four gospels are the heart of all the Scriptures. The gospels were formed in a three-part process.

[31] First, we have the life and teaching of Jesus. During his lifetime he gave example, he taught, and he gathered with others in community. The events of Jesus' life and the many things he taught us are the basis now of our own lives of discipleship.

[32] Second, after his death, an oral tradition developed as his followers told the story of Jesus to others. These stories not only expressed the remembered events from the life of Christ, but were also enlightened because the storytellers experienced the risen Lord in their midst.

[33] Finally, after some time had passed, the stories were collected into what we now call the four gospels. They were actually written down. In the writing, those early people of faith presented the stories of Jesus. Some of these stories helped explain the situation of their day, and some parts of the early Scriptures were part of their prayer life as a church.

WE BELIEVE

The unity of the Old and New Testaments demonstrates God's plan. The Old Testament prepares for the New, and the New Testament fulfills the Old. The two shed light on each other.

[34] For us Christians, the gospels hold pride of place in everything ever written, whether within the Bible or not. They are central to our faith.

[35] St. Thérèse of Lisieux reflected on this in her autobiography: "But above all it's the gospels that occupy my mind, when I'm at

prayer," she wrote; "my poor soul has so many needs, and yet this is the one thing needful. I'm always finding fresh lights there; hidden meanings which had meant nothing to me hitherto." Indeed, we find "fresh lights" in the gospels, and we grow to love them with all our hearts.

[36] Taken together, then, the Old and New Testaments should be read as complementary to one another. The New Testament is hidden in the Old, and the Old Testament is made plain in the New. We want everyone to read and pray the sacred Scriptures!

WE BELIEVE

The Church has always venerated the Scriptures just as we venerate the Body of Christ. Both nourish and sustain the Christian life.

---

[37] Once again turning to the *Constitution on Divine Revelation* from Vatican II, we get a sense of the Church's desire for us: "And such is the force and power of the word of God that it is the Church's support and strength" (article 21).

[38] And again, "Therefore, let them go gladly to the sacred text itself, whether in the sacred liturgy...or in devout reading" (article 25). The Church "forcefully and specifically exhorts all the Christian faithful...to learn the 'surpassing knowledge of Jesus Christ,' by frequent reading of the divine Scriptures" (article 25). For as St. Jerome reminds us, "Ignorance of the Scriptures is ignorance of Christ."

Group or personal process

- Go back to the list of books that appear in the Old and New Testaments. Circle those that are familiar to you.

- From the Old Testament, which stories do you know best? Are they well known to you because you have read and studied them or because you have heard them proclaimed at Mass or because you have seen these stories told in the movies?

- Which stories in the New Testament are favorites of yours?

- How have these stories touched your life or called you to conversion?

- How does the teaching in faith statement #35 touch your own heart and lead you to appreciate prayer with Scripture?

Prayer

Jesus, our encounter with you in the texts of sacred Scripture helps us understand your teachings and embrace your way of life. Help us become the disciples you have called us to be. Create new hearts within us, and guide us to know your will for us and for the world around us. As we offer you the work of our hands in today's world, we thank you for the power of your Holy Spirit. We pray in your holy name. Amen.

Session Three

....

BASED ON ARTICLES 198–227 OF THE *CATECHISM OF THE CATHOLIC CHURCH*. TO READ A SUMMARY OF THIS SECTION, SEE *CATECHISM* ARTICLES 228–231

Introduction

Having considered the power and place of Scripture in our lives and the life of the Church, we now turn to the nature of God in himself. What is God like? How does God behave toward us in the human family? What does God desire for all of creation? We begin by saying that God is love. In that simple phrase, we find the deepest meaning of human life. God is not human, not limited, not arbitrary or capricious, not even either male or female. God is just God. In the exciting relationship that results from God reaching out to us, we learn God's name. It is YHWH, which means, I AM. God just is. And while this is a great mystery, our faith helps us understand enough for now.

Scripture

READER: A reading from the Gospel of Mark.

One of the scribes came near and heard them disputing with one another, and seeing that he answered them well, he asked him, "Which commandment is the first of all?" Jesus answered, "The first is, 'Hear, O Israel: the Lord our God, the Lord is one; you shall love the Lord your God with all your heart, and with all your soul, and with all your mind, and with all your strength.' The second is this, 'You shall love your neighbor as yourself.' There is no other commandment greater than these." (MARK 12:28–31)

READER: The word of the Lord.

ALL: Thanks be to God.

PART ONE + *ARTICLES 198–205 OF THE CATECHISM*
What is God like?

[1] When we Christians recite our Creed, we begin by affirming that we believe in God. Belief in God is the foundation of everything else in which we profess our faith.

[2] Our entire Creed is fundamentally about God, and even when we speak of ourselves it is only in terms of our relationship with God. Even the first commandment begins with a declaration about God: "I am the Lord, your God..."

[3] We believe that there is only one God, and we aren't the first to believe this. It's part of our ancient heritage of faith. Even though we Christians speak of the Trinity, we always mean to say that God, the divine nature, the divine essence, the divine being, is one.

[4] The people of Israel believe this with us Christians. This shared faith in one God is perhaps the greatest legacy we have received from the Jewish people. But it is more than a legacy! We share that same faith even today. We worship and listen to the same God.

[5] And this faith is shared as well by the people of Islam. As a religion, Islam has the firm belief in one God at its very core.

[6] And our belief in God is not based on fiction or on wishful thinking or on human invention; it's based on God's own revelation to us. In Deuteronomy we read what may be the most famous declaration of faith ever written. It's in chapter 6, verse 4: "Hear, O Israel: The LORD is our God, the LORD alone." This simple statement of belief is the underpinning of all our faith.

[7] Jesus himself quotes this line in chapter 12, verse 29 of Mark's gospel. When we profess faith in Jesus Christ and call him Lord, or when we acclaim the Holy Spirit as the Lord and Giver of Life, we do not compromise our deep faith in one God.

[8] Indeed, we firmly profess that *we believe in one God*.

What is God's name?

[9] As we said earlier we are able to believe because God revealed to us God's own self. In human friendship, sharing our name with others is a first step on the road to intimacy. Sharing our name leads to us being able to call one another and know one another. It becomes a symbol of our whole selves to others.

[10] Likewise with God. God revealed God's own name to us. God actually revealed to us more than one divine name but the name that

proved to be most important is the one God revealed to Moses just as he was accepting his vocation.

[11] It came from the midst of a burning bush on the eve of the great exodus and just before the covenant reached on Sinai. "I am the God of your father," God told Moses, and then he called Moses to a wild and wonderful journey. The account of this is found in the Book of Exodus, chapter 3.

[12] And Moses, standing there on that holy ground, sandals off and face hidden, heard the compassionate God whom he loved promise to deliver the people of Israel to freedom and to give them a land flowing with milk and honey.

[13] Despite this dramatic calling in a dramatic setting from the midst of this burning bush, Moses still seemed unsure. "If I come to the Israelites and say to them, 'The God of your ancestors has sent me to you,' and they ask me, 'What is his name?' what shall I say to them?" Moses asked.

[14] Then God revealed to Moses his most personal name. "God said to Moses, I AM WHO I AM." Tell them, God said, "I AM has sent me to you...This is my name forever."

Group or personal process

• How has your understanding of God changed over the years—childhood, teen, young adult, adult, senior?

• How has that evolving understanding affected your conversation, reflections, and prayer life in terms of the names you use for God? How intimate is your name for God?

- Read faith statements #10–14 again. Why do you think God was so eager to have us meet and know him?

The divine mystery

[15] What a mysterious name! In Hebrew it is rendered, simply, YHWH. But what does this name mean? It is at once a revelation and a mystery. God is the one who is close enough to us humans to share the divine name with us, and yet no one can ever plumb the depths of the divine mystery.

[16] So we are at once close to God and yet we hold God in the greatest esteem. "God is greater than our hearts," we read in the First Letter of John, chapter 3, verse 20, "and God knows everything."

[17] And because of the great esteem in which the people of Israel held God, they did not pronounce God's name aloud. It was simply too awesome and holy! In Scripture, the revealed name, YHWH, is replaced by what is really a divine title, LORD. Hence, Jesus is called LORD.

[18] Guided by God's pillar of light and commissioned as God's agent, Moses led the Israelites out of Egypt. And the LORD remained with them, even when they sinned and turned away. And likewise with us. The LORD is endlessly forgiving and endlessly loving toward us.

[19] In Jesus Christ we experience this God in God's most amazing form. Down through the years our understanding of God has grown

and become richer and deeper. We have come to understand that God is unique and there are no other gods.

[20] God is the creator of heaven and earth and will endure forever above history and beyond the world. God does not change and is always faithful and true, without beginning or end, eternal, the source of all life, all being, and all that is.

WE BELIEVE

God remains a mystery to us even though he has revealed himself. The mystery is one of depth, not of misunderstanding or confusion. We simply cannot plumb the depths of God.

---

[21] Above all, God loves us with the tenderness of a parent for a child. God is steadfast in love; he is constant and faithful in calling us to love with the same fidelity. "God is love," we read in the First Letter of John, chapter 4, verse 16, "and those who abide in love abide in God and God abides in them."

God is truth

[22] God's promises are real, and God does not deceive, for God is truth itself. For this reason, we humans can trust in God and rely upon the divine word. Because God is creator of heaven and earth, only in God do we find wisdom, and only in God do we find the pathway by which we come to understand life's meaning.

[23] In the Gospel of John, chapter 18, verse 37, we read that Jesus reflected this profound mystery in himself. Pilate is questioning Jesus about his mission and asks him whether or not he is a king. We're in the moments just before Jesus is sentenced to death in the heart of John's passion story. "For this I was born," Jesus tells

Pilate—and us—"for this I came into the world: to testify to the truth. Everyone who belongs to the truth listens to my voice."

Group or personal process

- How have you experienced the mercy, love, and faithfulness of God in your life?

- How have you experienced doubt about God's presence, or doubt that God is love?

- How does the story told in faith statement #23 help you understand how God works in Christ and in our own lives?

- What helps you grow in your faith? What hinders that growth?

PART THREE + **ARTICLES 218–227 OF THE** *CATECHISM*
God is love

[24] What is most amazing about this whole divine story of God creating the world and us, of God sharing the divine name with us, and of God remaining faithfully with us, is the motive. It is not a motive of power, or of fame, or of wealth, or of influence, or any other such motive.

[25] It is a pure, single motive, one that we may find hard to imagine or understand. God behaves toward us as God does out of sheer, freely given *love*. God's love is almost overwhelming! "You are precious in my sight...," God tells us through Isaiah in chapter 43, verse

4, "and I love you." It nearly takes your breath away to hear it!

[26] More than a mom or dad can love their child, so much does God love us! And out of that great love for the world and us, God shared intimately with us by giving us Jesus Christ, the only Son of God, as we read in John's gospel.

WE BELIEVE
God has revealed himself to us just as he is, abounding in love, mercy, and faithfulness. God's very being is Truth and Love.

[27] In chapter 54 of Isaiah we have this assurance: even if the mountains were swept away and the hills disappeared, *even then*, "my steadfast love shall not depart from you..."

[28] And in chapter 31 of Jeremiah, we read this promise: "I have loved you with an everlasting love; therefore I have continued my faithfulness to you."

[29] Then in the gospels we come to understand that God not only loves us but that God is the very being of love itself. This is the secret of the mystery of God revealed forever through Christ: God is the eternal sharing of the very same love that we are destined to share with each other.

What does this mean for us?
[30] Placing our faith in God, the one, true God, and the God who is love, changes our lives completely. First and foremost, faith leads us to recognize God in greatness, beauty, generosity, and love.

[31] Second, faith creates within us grateful hearts and a desire to respond in turn by being generous, forgiving, and merciful ourselves.

[32] Third, faith leads us to see the basic unity of all humankind and the dignity of every human person, all created in God's own image.

[33] Fourth, faith leads us to see all creation as holy, precious, and useful only to lead us to God. When material things lead us away from God or become an end in themselves for us, then faith leads us to detach from them and turn our hearts back to the divine.

[34] And finally, faith leads us to trust God in every single situation in life, even when times are bad.

Group or personal process

- As you think about it, what have we humans not yet fully understood about what God wants for us? Read faith statement #27 again as you reflect on this.

- How have we failed to live up to our destiny as children of God? What would you suggest we do to become more faithful?

Prayer

Father, throughout the ages you have offered us a relationship with you. Even when we remained selfish, when we failed to live with the self-giving love that you have implanted in our hearts, you reached out to offer us a covenant. We now turn our hearts back to you once again, ready and willing to be your sons and daughters. We open ourselves to your love and forgiveness. Strengthen us and increase our faith. We pray through Christ, our Lord. Amen.

Session Four

BASED ON ARTICLES 232–260 OF THE *CATECHISM OF THE CATHOLIC CHURCH*. TO READ A SUMMARY OF THIS SECTION, SEE *CATECHISM* ARTICLES 261–267

Introduction

We have not yet said all we need to about God. In the last session, we only touched on the surface of this wonder and mystery. Now we turn to consider the Blessed Trinity. In our own frail and inadequate human way, we say that we believe in one God. We assert that God alone is the origin of life and our ultimate goal. This means that we are born of God, that we live in God, and that we return to God as our destiny. Do we understand this fully? No, we do not. For even when God reveals God's self, God remains a mystery beyond words. The mystery of the Trinity is the central Christian mystery. God is three in one: Father, Son, and Holy Spirit. When we live in love ourselves, we also share the life of this Blessed Trinity.

Scripture

READER: A reading from the Gospel of John.

"When the Spirit of truth comes, he will guide you into all the truth; for he will not speak on his own, but will speak whatever he hears, and he will declare to you the things that are to come. He will glorify me, because he will take what is mine and declare it to you. All that the Father has is mine. For this reason I said that he will take what is mine and declare it to you." (JOHN 16:13–15)

READER: The word of the Lord.

ALL: Thanks be to God.

PART ONE ✦ **ARTICLES 232–239 OF THE *CATECHISM***
The basis of our faith

[1] This is a story about love: tremendous, powerful, life-changing love. At baptism a Christian is signed in the name of the Father, and of the Son, and of the Holy Spirit. The cross of Christ is traced on our bodies as we profess this faith, and all we believe rests on this.

[2] That cross and our belief in God results only from God's love for us. We give a name to this wonderful and mysterious belief: we call it *The Most Holy Trinity.*

[3] And it is mystery. But it is a mystery of depth, not of misunderstanding. For who can plumb the depths of God? Who can know the heart of the LORD? Indeed, it is *the* central Christian mystery, and among Christian beliefs it is the most central and important. All that we believe can be summed up in this one mystery.

[4] We want to consider this because of its importance: how the Trinity was revealed by God to us, how the Church received and expressed the revelation, and how we understand the words and deeds of God, undertaken by the Father, Son, and Spirit.

[5] For these deeds and words are how God's plan of loving goodness toward us is carried out in what we have come to see as a "threefold manner." We might even call this threefold manner by another name: Creating, Redeeming, and Sanctifying.

---

[6] But what we believe is beyond mere deeds and words, because what has been revealed to us as the threefold manner of God being among us also reveals God's innermost life, God's way of being.

[7] This latter revelation, that of God's inner life, sheds light on our understanding of the deeds and words. Just as any human person tells who he or she really is more by how he or she acts than by what he or she says, so with God. God's actions in word and deed tell us about God.

[8] So we search among God's actions to find traces of the inner life of God hidden there.

Jesus reveals his Father

[9] Many religions use the human title of Father to refer to God. They do this, not because they think God, who is above and beyond human biological life, is actually a male, or actually a father, but because our language has no other title that fits quite as well.

[10] By using the title Father, we are saying two important things. First, we are saying that God is the origin of life, and, second, we are saying that God is full of goodness and loving care for us all.

WE BELIEVE

Jesus came to live among us, which demonstrates how God is the eternal Father. We believe that Jesus and the Father are consubstantial, meaning they are one and the same God.

---

[11] We might also express this through the image of Mother, as the *Catechism* reminds us in article 239, which gives emphasis to the intimacy between Creator and creature. This is the language of faith, and we can only draw on what we humans know and how we experience love, intimacy, and birth.

[12] But our experience also tells us that parents can fail. They can be downright un-parent-like. So it is important to remember that God transcends all this. God is neither male nor female; God is just God.

Group or personal process

- The *Catechism* takes care to help us see that God is not human, even though we use human titles and names to address God. With what name do you address God most of the time?

- How does this shape your prayer?

- Read faith statement #11 again and possibly read it in the *Catechism* itself. How do images of God play a role in your prayer life?

- Using your Bible, choose one of the gospel accounts and find there the various ways that Jesus refers to God using metaphor, image, and parable. Write these down and share them with another person.

PART TWO + **ARTICLES 240–252 OF THE** *CATECHISM*

The Trinity of love

[13] In Jesus we learn more. God is in eternal relationship to Christ as a Son, and likewise, Christ to God as a Father. The Gospel of John in its very opening lines expresses this in another way: "In the beginning was the Word, and the Word was with God, and the Word was God."

[14] Based on this, the Creed was written at the Councils of Nicaea in 325 and Constantinople in 381. The words composed there are similar to ones we pray today each time we profess our faith using that Creed.

[15] We say that Jesus is "the Only Begotten Son of God, born of the Father before all ages. God from God, Light from Light, true God from true God, begotten, not made, consubstantial with the Father."

The Spirit reveals the Trinity
[16] In chapter 14, the Gospel of John records a wonderful speech that Christ gave to his followers, and therefore to us, on the eve of his arrest. "I will ask the Father," he tells us, "and he will give you another Advocate, to be with you forever. This is the Spirit of truth..."

[17] Thus, the Holy Spirit is revealed as another person within the divine being along with Jesus and the Father. Here we now have revealed to us God's threefold inner life, present from the beginning, acting among us out of love, and thereby revealing God to us.

[18] The Council at Constantinople (mentioned above) also wrote words for the Creed about the Spirit. "I believe in the Holy Spirit," they wrote, "the Lord, the giver of life, who proceeds from the Father."

[19] Later, this would become the firm belief in the West that the Spirit proceeds from the Father *and the Son.* The Holy Spirit was sent by God at the word of Christ and is the Spirit of both. It is the Spirit of God.

[20] Indeed, the Creed puts it this way: "With the Father and the Son, [he is] adored and glorified."

Understanding the Trinity

[21] Since the earliest years of the Church and since the very early writing of Church leaders, a sense of the Trinity has been present. For example, in his greetings to fellow Christians, St. Paul wrote to those living in Corinth, "The grace of the Lord Jesus Christ and the love of God and the fellowship of the Holy Spirit be with you all."

[22] This early faith was then systematically clarified at several early Church councils including the two mentioned above. During this time, the Church was careful to express what people actually believed and what the Church believed to be revealed.

[23] In doing this, the Church used certain terms giving them a new and significant meaning. These terms are usually the stuff of theology and formal study. It should always be remembered that God is

mystery and that we humans really can never adequately explain or even express very well the inner life of God.

WE BELIEVE

By the grace received in baptism, we share in the life of the Blessed Trinity. We are baptized "in the name of the Father, and of the Son, and of the Holy Spirit."

[24] Nonetheless, the Church uses three important words: (a) "substance" (also "essence" or "nature") refers to the unity within the inner life of God; (b) "person" refers to trinity of persons within God's inner life: Father, Son, and Spirit; (c) "relation" refers to the distinct ways these persons are related to one another.

Group or personal process

- How do you experience the presence of God in your life under this threefold manner:
  Father: creator, and source of life;
  Son: Lord, and redeeming example of self-giving love;
  Holy Spirit: source of holiness, truth, and wisdom?

- How does the teaching in faith statement #16 help you understand the role of the Holy Spirit?

One God

[25] It's terribly important to note that we do not believe in three gods, but in one God in three persons living together in Trinity. So each of these three persons is God, whole and entire, sharing one divine nature.

[26] But the divine persons are also really distinct from one another. It isn't merely that we designate different ways in which they act, but that we designate distinct persons within the inner life of God.

WE BELIEVE

Our Catholic faith rests on our belief in one God in the Trinity and the Trinity in unity. Each person of the Trinity is distinct yet all three are one.

---

[27] The key to this is to understand that God is love and that the loving energy of God is present in the person of Father, in the person of the Son who became incarnate, and in the person of the Holy Spirit: One God in three loving persons related to each other and wholly present in one another.

[28] All the work of creation, all the patient love down through the centuries, all the work of Jesus Christ, and all the sanctifying work of the Spirit—all of it emerges as the common work of the three persons within the Trinity.

[29] Each divine person performs the common work according to each one's unique properties of creation, redemption, and sanctification.

[30] For the Christian, understanding and living with the Trinity means paying attention to the work of the Trinity within our own lives. It means knowing God intimately and living in communion with God.

[31] We can grow to think of ourselves (as John's gospel suggests in chapter 14) as a dwelling for the Trinity, God making a divine home within us.

Group or personal process

- We shared above how *we experience God*. Now share about how in your everyday life you are yourself an expression of the Trinity for others—as creative, as saving, and as making holy? In other words, share about how other people experience God *through* you?

- Share a prayer of your own expressing your faith in the Blessed Trinity.

Prayer

O God, in Christ you revealed yourself to us, and in your Spirit you continue to help us encounter you. In your threefold presence, you reveal love to us, implant it within our hearts, and help us become loving men and women. With all our hearts we turn to you; we open ourselves to your presence and listen for your word, which is spoken in the depths of our souls. May your love move the whole world to works of justice, peace, and goodness. We pray to you in the name of your Son and through the power of the Holy Spirit. Amen.

Session Five

GOD, THE CREATOR

....

BASED ON ARTICLES 268–274 AND 279–314 OF THE *CATECHISM OF THE CATHOLIC CHURCH*. TO READ A SUMMARY OF THIS SECTION, SEE *CATECHISM* ARTICLES 275–278 AND 315–324

Introduction

Having probed the depths of the mystery of the Blessed Trinity, let us now turn to consider the deeds of God in the creation of the world and all its creatures. In the creation of the world and of us, God gave the first and universal witness to God's almighty love and wisdom. God created out of love and for no other reason. We believe that God alone created the universe freely, directly, and without any help. And we believe that God keeps us and the entire universe in existence through Jesus Christ, in whom all things continue in being, and by the Spirit, the giver of life. In the midst of all this beauty and love, however, evil does exist and we have all experienced it; for us, this is another facet of the mystery of God.

Scripture

READER: A reading from the Book of Genesis.

In the beginning when God created the heavens and the earth, the earth was a formless void and darkness covered the face of the deep, while a wind from God swept over the face of the waters. Then God said, "Let there be light"; and there was light. And God saw that the light was good; and God separated the light from the darkness. God called the light Day, and the darkness he called Night. And there was evening and there was morning, the first day. (GENESIS 1:1–5)

READER: The word of the Lord.

ALL: Thanks be to God.

PART ONE + ARTICLES 268–274 AND 279–281 OF THE *CATECHISM*
Holy power

[1] Of all the various ways we describe God, none is more central than our belief that God is love. The First Letter of John presents this belief in a powerful way in chapter 4: "God is love," it says, "and those who abide in love abide in God..."

[2] God is therefore the energy or power of love realized in the world and in creation. But it is important to note that God is not a person in the same way that you and I are persons. When we use the word "person" to describe ourselves, we mean that we are in a specific place at a certain moment in history; we have limited knowledge, limited abilities, and limited lifetimes; a person can be arbitrary, capricious, or even mean; persons have gender—either male or female; and in the end, of course, every person eventually dies.

[3] When we speak of God as a person, we don't mean any of these things. God is not limited by space and time; God is not limited in knowledge or abilities: God is all-knowing and all-powerful; God is not arbitrary or capricious toward us: God is constant; God is not male or female; and, of course, God does not die.

[4] When we describe God as we do, we're merely using feeble hu-

man language to describe the awesome power of love. And sometimes when we do this, we accidentally push God away from us, making God seem distant or removed.

[5] We come dangerously close then to believing in the false god that Jesus corrects in our understanding.

WE BELIEVE

We in the Church address our prayer to "Almighty God" because we believe firmly that with God, nothing is impossible.

---

[6] As we have said many times, God is love. God gives us the power of love. God moves us with grace and empowers us through it. When we speak of divine power in this way, we do not mean to suggest the kind of unilateral power humans often desire.

[7] God's isn't a power used to dominate or "lord it over others" but just the opposite. *Again, it is the power of God.*

[8] We believe that God contains (within the Trinity) the secret to life and happiness. This is the great mystery that when we give ourselves in love as God gives to us, *we are made whole.* When we die to ourselves, we rise again in new life. A great mystery.

[9] The Bible repeatedly returns to this theme. Throughout the Old Testament the LORD is known as mighty, strong, and maker of heaven and earth. God is the holy order-bringer, and from it, the universe flows.

[10] As the author of love, God reveals the divine plan and communicates the divine heart to us. God's mercy is infinite, and his forgiveness is endless. In this way weakness becomes strength, and we are saved in ways we do not realize we need to be.

[11] And because the divine power is expressed in love, it is always just. It always flows from wisdom. We humans struggle sometimes to understand how weakness is powerful, but such weakness is, in fact, the divine way.

WE BELIEVE

In his powerful way, God converts us from our sin
and restores us to friendship with him.

[12] Throughout the teachings of Christ and in all the ways God works, the first are last, the downtrodden are raised up, enemies are forgiven, Christ is crucified—but (and here is the mystery) in all of this God reigns.

[13] God is impossible to understand for those who wish to apply science to God, or to understand God according to the human heart. Only faith can embrace the mysterious ways of the almighty power of God. In faith we celebrate the weakness of love, that is, the giving of ourselves to others and the service which is characteristic of the Christian.

[14] As Mary sang in her beautiful song of faith in chapter 1 of the Gospel of Luke, "[God] has looked with favor on the lowliness of his servant." And yet, mysteriously, precisely because of love's weakness, love is strong and nothing is impossible to God. And this is the reason we pray in our Creed, "I believe in one God, the Father almighty..."

Group or personal process

- Have you ever seen how weakness can become strength?

- Have you experienced or have you heard of instances in which love is stronger than hate?

- How do faith statements #6 and #7 lead you to understand God as love?

- Whom do you know who exercises power in the likeness of God?

PART TWO + **ARTICLES 282–301 OF THE** *CATECHISM*

The Creator

[15] The Book of Genesis, the first book of the Bible, begins with these words: "In the beginning God created the heavens and the earth." Our faith also begins with this: God provides us with the generous and free gift of creation.

[16] God is eternal, but creation and the world are not. They occur within history, within time, and with a beginning and an end. And they are part of how God "shares love with others," we might say.

[17] They burst forth from the Trinity, from the intense love generated there. And it is for this reason that we begin great feasts by reading once again the accounts of creation that inspire awe.

Understanding creation

[18] We humans have always wondered about life: its origin and

end. Where do we come from? And where are we going? Science can help us, and indeed all our scientific study about the world—the aspects of the universe and cosmos, the emergence of life forms in ancient times, and the appearance of humans in the midst of this—only serves to deepen our awe and increase our gratitude to God.

[19] But there is a deeper question as well, and it revolves around the *meaning* of all creation. Is creation really only an accident of evolution, as some might argue, or is it truly the action of a loving divine being?

WE BELIEVE

God showed his almighty love for us by creating the world and us in that love. This is the first proclamation of God's plan of loving goodness for the world. Its goal was reached in Christ.

---

[20] And if it is the latter, then why are there evil, suffering, and pain? Down through the centuries we humans have answered this "meaning question" in a variety of ways. There have been numerous philosophies and theologies, numerous theories about life and the world.

[21] And isn't it just like us humans to question like this? Faith leads us Christians to assurance about creation because in faith we recognize the hand of God. Down through the centuries, God has revealed the truth about creation, life, death, sin, and suffering.

[22] So revelation about creation is connected closely to revelation about our covenant with God and revelation about God's powerful love. Even a brief, cursory reading of Scripture helps us grasp this divine revelation.

[23] Among all the biblical texts about creation, the first three chapters of the Book of Genesis occupy a unique place. Even though these texts come from differing sources, the authors were inspired, we believe, to express through them what God reveals, namely, that God's divine hand shapes the order and goodness of creation.

WE BELIEVE

*God alone created the universe, working
in the Trinity and without any help.*

---

[24] We believe that all creation flows from God the Father: freely, generously, and lovingly. Likewise, creation is the work of Christ the Son, the Word that was in the beginning and through whom all things were made. And again, it flows from the Spirit, who is called Lord and giver of life.

[25] In sum, we might say it like this: God who is Creator and author of life made all things by divine Word and Wisdom and gave them holy order. Hence, creation is the shared work of the Trinity. And what a glorious creation it is!

[26] God creates and is still creating as a profound way to demonstrate how to love. We were all created from this energy or power of love, and this is the whole reason for creation. We are destined to be children of the Triune God: sons and daughters. This destiny is clear in the mission of Christ.

[27] So we must live life fully, celebrate God's creative love, love each other as sisters and brothers, seek peace and justice, follow God's will of love, and allow ourselves to be immersed in God. This is how we give glory to God; this is how we live as we are meant to.

[28] We humans are intended for love and for a share in divine wisdom and goodness. God made all this wisdom, goodness, light, and the world itself from nothing. Likewise, from God flow forgiveness and a fresh heart for those who choose initially not to live by God's plan.

[29] Just as the light shining in the darkness flows from love, so God gives the light of faith to those who do not yet have it. Because creation is God's handiwork, it demonstrates to us what God is like. And in it we find great hope! For we find holy order, tremendous goodness, great plenty, and stunning beauty.

[30] Only when we fail to live according to our destiny and destroy or misuse creation does it become ugly and disfigured.

WE BELIEVE

God keeps the universe in existence by the power of his Word and Spirit. In Christ, all things continue in being, and it is the Spirit who is the giver of life.

Ongoing creation

[31] Creation, of course, is ongoing and not yet fully complete. God continues to be with us as we humans and the world unfold. Hence, God sustains life, upholds it, and enables us to live according to our destiny.

[32] We are, in a word, utterly dependent upon God, but this dependence brings with it only trust, freedom, joy, and confidence. For God is within all creation and will remain with us forever.

Group or personal process

- How would you describe our destiny and purpose as human beings?

- How do you live according to this purpose in your own life?

- How do you experience God continuing to guide us as we discover new medicines, new ideas, advances in science, and new corners of the universe?

PART THREE + ARTICLES 302–314 OF THE *CATECHISM*

The journey of creation

[33] As we just said above, creation is still underway and is still flowing from God. We believe that creation is in what we call "a state of journeying," which is a lovely way of saying that God is guiding the world to ultimate fulfillment.

[34] The energy of God, let us say once again, remains with us humans and the world as we journey through time to perfect unity and God's presence. When we discover a new medicine, when a track star sets a new record in the long jump, when we reach the moon or the stars, when we dialogue our way to peace, when we unfold new mysteries of life, God is with us and is "the author" of that work.

[35] Hence, God "takes care of us," we might say, as we journey together. It is plain to see from this that there is a role for us humans in creation. We can cooperate in the divine unfolding, and when we do, great things happen! In the account of creation that we read

in Genesis, we humans became partners with each other and also with all creation.

[36] We are called to use our intellect, our freedom, and our energy to be a coworker with God in the unfolding of creation. Indeed, how could God not be present with us when we work and study and explore creation? Does not our very life flow from God? And does not love direct human progress and, in fact, set it all in motion?

WE BELIEVE

God guides the world through the hearts of men and women. Our ultimate end is unity and love in God.

---

[37] When we cut ourselves off from God and impose our own human standards, motives, and goals, evil results. Only when we truly live in the flow of God written into the very fabric of what is created, can we "hit the mark" and be all we are created to be.

Evil

[38] Why does evil exist, and from where does it come? This is not an easy question and there is no easy answer. And we cannot expect the answer we do achieve to be satisfactory or the final word on the matter. Indeed, humans have struggled with this question for many generations.

[39] To grasp it even a little, we must consider Christian faith as a whole. Every single aspect of our faith provides part of the answer to this question: how in our freedom we stray from love, how this leads us to a false sense of God, how God patiently calls us back, how Christ teaches us to be holy again, how Christ's dying and rising

opens the way, how the Church gathers for this purpose, and how the sacraments serve to sustain us. Each aspect of our faith helps us understand evil.

[40] One might wonder why, if God is indeed the energy that holds the world together, then why is the world so imperfect? Why does the world seem sometimes to spin out of control with evil, pain, suffering, war, and death? Not to mention earthquakes, fires, floods, and storms.

WE BELIEVE

The fact that God permits evil is a mystery that is illuminated by the life and death of Christ. God does not will evil but he does permit it, and we believe that good can come from that very evil. It is a mystery.

[41] Let us gently recall that creation is not completed and we are in that "state of journeying." The world is not yet complete but is on the path to wholeness or completeness. And we humans too are on a journey, sometimes acting selfishly and sometimes acting with love. Indeed, the moral evils we perpetrate and the sins we commit are far more harmful than storms and earthquakes.

[42] Because we are partners in creation with God and even in the work of salvation, we retain the freedom that allows us to sometimes be intentionally selfish and sinful. God made freedom part and parcel of being human in order to receive our freely given love. But even in the face of the worst moral evil, good can result because God remains with us even then.

[43] This returns us to the idea that weakness is really strength in the mystery of God. Can life come from death? Yes! Can grace result from sin? Yes! Can new wheat result from the death of a seed? Indeed, yes!

In conclusion

[44] St. Catherine of Siena once said to those who'd lost perspective and felt hopeless in the face of what was happening to them: "Everything comes from love; all is ordained for the salvation of [humans]; God does nothing without this goal in mind."

Group or personal process

- Name what you consider to be two or three serious or significant evils of our time.

- What great natural disasters can you recall?

- How do the teachings in faith statements #35 and #36 help you see more clearly your own role in today's world?

- Now pause, allow the presence of the Spirit to stir you, and find in these evils and disasters all the ways that goodness might result. How can goodness flow from evil and disaster?

Prayer

O God, you have looked with favor on us, your lowly servants.
You have created the world out of love and given it to us, asking us to
tend it as a garden. When we acted selfishly and sinfully, you offered
us a pathway back to your grace. Now we turn our hearts to you,
O God, by the power of your Spirit and in the name of your Son,
Jesus. Help us to become stewards of your earth, to share it wisely
and fairly with all, and to treat each other and all your creatures
with the dignity with which you created us. We pray through Christ,
our Lord. Amen.

Session Six

OUR GUIDE AND INSPIRATION: THE HOLY SPIRIT

BASED ON ARTICLES 683–741 OF THE *CATECHISM OF THE CATHOLIC CHURCH*. TO READ A SUMMARY OF THIS SECTION, SEE *CATECHISM* ARTICLES 742–747

Introduction

With the discussion on evil in the last session giving us a hint about what is to come when we consider sin, let us conclude our study of the mystery of God by considering what we believe about the Holy Spirit. Whenever God sends Christ, he always sends the Spirit: their mission is conjoined and inseparable. So the Spirit is with us all the time, as it has been with the prophets, martyrs, and teachers of the Church. In the fullness of time, the Holy Spirit completed in Mary all the preparations for Christ's coming among the People of God. In her yes, God came to live among us as Emmanuel. And the Holy Spirit, whom Christ sends, now builds, animates, and makes holy we who are the Church, the People of God. In fact, the Church is the sacrament or sign to the world of the Holy Trinity's communion with us.

Scripture

READER: A reading from the First Letter of Paul to the Corinthians.

Now there are varieties of gifts, but the same Spirit; and there are varieties of services, but the same Lord; and there are varieties of activities, but it is the same God who activates all of them in everyone. To each is given the manifestation of the Spirit for the common good. (1 Corinthians 12:4–7)

READER: The word of the Lord.

ALL: Thanks be to God.

PART ONE ✛ *ARTICLES 683–694 OF THE CATECHISM*

God

[1] "Those who bear God's Spirit," St. Irenaeus once wrote, "are led to the Word." It is the Spirit, we believe, the Spirit of God, otherwise known as the Holy Spirit, who first makes belief possible in our hearts.

[2] We believe the Spirit of God lives within the Holy Trinity. The Holy Trinity—Father, Son, and Holy Spirit—is one God.

[3] From the beginning, it has been this same God providing words and deeds that created the world and us people. God journeyed with us down through the centuries, revealing the divine heart to us completely through the Son of God and remaining with us as source of wisdom, truth, power, and help in the Spirit. The great love that flows from the Trinity comes always from one God.

[4] It is the Spirit who opens our hearts and forms our innermost being to receive Christ and to know Christ and to share Christ in community. And in knowing Christ, we know God himself. Indeed, for us humans, it is the Trinitarian experience of God that empowers us.

The works of the Spirit

[5] The world neither sees nor knows the Spirit, according to John's gospel, but we can plainly recognize the work of the Spirit: sacred Scripture is written under the guidance of the Spirit, and Tradition is likewise guided by the same Spirit.

[6] The teaching offices of the Church depend upon this Spirit, and it is the Spirit who puts us into communion with Christ. In prayer, it is the Spirit who opens our hearts, gives us gifts for the good of the world, and provides words of witness. As we said above, the love of the Trinity is inseparable and always works as one God.

[7] And the really glorious part of this story is that we who are baptized into Christ are anointed by the Spirit. And in that Spirit we become adopted children of God.

WE BELIEVE

From the beginning to the end of time, whenever God sends Jesus Christ, his Son, he also sends the Spirit. Their mission in the world is one mission.

How we name the Spirit

[8] We give a name to the Spirit of God and that name is Holy Spirit, a name that conjures up images of breath, air, and wind. The sense that the Spirit is the breath of God and stirs up within us a whirlwind of God is very strong in the gospels.

[9] Jesus promises this Spirit to us using the name Spirit of truth, and we have a strong tradition of understanding that it is this truth that sets us free, liberation being at the heart of Jesus' mission.

[10] Jesus also refers to this Spirit as Advocate, which means Helper. Other names are also applied to the Spirit throughout the

New Testament but all of them refer to one and the same Spirit of God.

Holy water

[11] Our initiation into the Church, which comes to us at baptism, occurs under the symbol of water. When the woman at the well in chapter 4 of John's gospel asked Jesus for a drink of water, he told her that the water he would give, unlike the water in that well, would become in her "a spring of water gushing up to eternal life."

Group or personal process

- How do you experience the Spirit of God working in your life?

- Read faith statement #6 again. How does the Spirit empower your own faith?

- We must discern the voice of God when it echoes in our depths to be certain it is the Holy Spirit we hear calling us. When the call is to love and goodness, we can trust it is God speaking. How and when have you heard this voice of God echoing in the depths of your heart?

PART TWO **+ ARTICLES 695–716 OF THE *CATECHISM***

Holy anointing

[12] It is likewise in the Spirit that we are anointed in confirmation. The word "Christ" means literally "the one anointed by God's

Spirit." It is Christ who now gives that Spirit to us. Christ is the minister of confirmation, with the bishop acting on Christ's behalf.

[13] When we speak of Christ and the Spirit separately like this, it is only to distinguish their unique roles; but, in fact, we believe they are inseparable and always act as one God.

Holy fire
[14] Here we come to an experience of Spirit that has the power to set the world on fire! The Spirit of God is powerful, the *most* powerful force of all, which alone can renew the face of the earth.

[15] "Come, Holy Spirit," we pray, "fill the hearts of your faithful and kindle in them the fire of your love."

Holy light
[16] As we humans struggle with our feeble language and attempt to express our experience of Holy Spirit, one image that seems to speak to us is that of light. We are "enlightened" by the Spirit to recognize truth and to know Christ.

Holy hands
[17] When the ordained lay hands on one another to ordain and bless and heal, a powerful sign of the Spirit is expressed. Jesus himself healed the sick and blessed the children by laying hands on them.

Holy dove
[18] As a symbol of the Holy Spirit, the dove has symbolically appeared in our Scriptures to announce the end of the flood to Noah and to remain with Christ in power after his own baptism. And in sacred art the dove is a common symbol representing the presence of God's Spirit.

The Spirit in the Old Testament

[19] We believe the Spirit of God has spoken throughout history: from the time of Genesis and Exodus through the prophets and the wisdom writings and right up to John the Baptist. In the symbolic language of the creation stories of Genesis, it was the Spirit of God that hovered over the chaos and that was breathed into our nostrils. Being formed in the image of God is being formed in the image of the Spirit.

[20] And then from Abraham and Sarah, through Isaac and Rebecca, to Moses and Miriam, to Joshua and the visions of the prophets, the Spirit of God has been present. This Spirit, we believe, is in the law, and obeying the law of God yields a life in the Spirit. But to fall away from the law of love, to be unfaithful to our created purpose, ends in death.

WE BELIEVE

The Spirit has guided the People of God from the beginning. The Son of God was consecrated as Christ or Messiah by the anointing of the Spirit.

----

[21] Perhaps this Old Testament work of the Spirit came to a peak in the prophet Isaiah, where, in chapter 11, we read: "A shoot shall come out from the stump of Jesse, and a branch shall grow out of his roots. The Spirit of the Lord shall rest on him, the spirit of wisdom and understanding, the spirit of counsel and might, the spirit of knowledge and fear of the Lord."

[22] Later, according to Luke, when Jesus of Nazareth was ready to begin his own ministry, he quoted from Isaiah, chapter 61: "The spirit of the Lord is upon me because he has anointed me to bring good news to the poor. He has sent me to proclaim release to the

captives and recovery of sight to the blind, to let the oppressed go free, to proclaim the year of the Lord's favor" (Luke 4:18–19).

Group or personal process

- Which sign of the Spirit speaks most powerfully to you?

- In your own words, what role does the Spirit play in our daily lives?

PART THREE + ARTICLES 717–741 OF THE *CATECHISM*
The Spirit in the New Testament

[23] And then, in due time, there was John the Baptist who, as the text of Luke tells us, was filled with the Holy Spirit. There is consistent belief in our Scriptures that John was "a witness who came to testify to the light." In him, the Spirit of God completes the preparations for Christ the anointed one.

[24] In Mary, the Spirit of God brings to life the revelation of love: Christ, the Lord. The Spirit of God's love flowed through Mary as grace, keeping her heart in love always and never in selfishness and sin.

[25] And finally, through her powerful and loving heart came the Christ, the Son of God, and lo! Emmanuel! God is with us! Jesus of Nazareth, as we have already seen, lived and worked only in the power of the Spirit.

[26] We must always remember, when we think about this, that God is revealed in Christ, the Son of God; and our own hearts are

enlightened to believe by the power of the Spirit. In this, God always acts in word and deed as one God.

[27] The gospels do not give a clear portrait of Jesus and his understanding of the Spirit. While the Gospel of John is rich in texts that underscore the work of the Spirit, other gospels give scant mention. John's gospel, written several generations after the resurrection, may provide a theology of the Spirit's work but not a biographical account of Jesus' life.

WE BELIEVE

In Mary, the Spirit completes the preparation for Christ's arrival among us. Through the Spirit's action in Mary's heart, God gave the world Emmanuel, "God-with-us" (Mt 1:23).

[28] Reading this theology, we have come to understand that the Spirit is our teacher and our trustworthy helper. The mission of the Church as the People of God, which is the same as the mission of Christ, is the same as that of the Spirit as well.

[29] The First Letter of John reminds us that "God is love." Indeed, God's love is never-ending; it is generous, forgiving, and constant. It is the understanding of the Church as expressed by Paul in Romans, chapter 5, that the first gift of the Spirit of God is love itself "poured into our hearts through the Holy Spirit who has been given to us."

[30] It is this love that restores us. It is this love that Jesus refused to surrender. It is this love that has God as its source. It is this love that the Spirit gives us.

[31] Speaking on behalf of the believing Church, the writer of the

First Letter of John provides a helpful commentary on this: "No one has ever seen God," the writer reminds us in chapter 4, verse 12; "if we love one another, God lives in us and [God's] love is perfected in us."

[32] The more we live in this love, the more we donate ourselves to others, the more we forgive over and over, the more we share our daily bread with the poor, the more we are patient, kind, faithful, and gentle of heart, the more we live in the Spirit.

WE BELIEVE

The Holy Spirit builds, animates, and makes holy the Church,
the sacrament of the Trinity's communion with the human family.

---

[33] The Church, then, as the body of Christ, is God's holy people walking together enlightened for faith by the Spirit. The Church, we might say, is primarily a sacrament bearing witness to all these truths, caring for the sick, rejected, and poor, living according to the teachings of Christ, and welcoming all into the power of love.

[34] It is a sacrament of the Trinity of God in communion with us all! We are not set side by side collectively as Church, but we are bound together by the same principle: the Spirit. Christ the Son of God releases into our own hearts the Spirit that so fills his own.

[35] Through the sacraments, Christ acts in our midst to unify, strengthen, heal, and, in short, make holy the members of the Church.

Group or personal process

- What works of the Spirit do you see around you?

- Read faith statements #31 and #32 again.
  What strikes you as most powerful in this teaching?

- In what ways can you cooperate more fully with the Spirit
  in your own life?

Prayer

O Holy Spirit, you are the fire in our hearts and the light in our
souls. By your power, we are led to believe, to work, and to pray as
we build the reign of God. In your presence, we are moved with
awe as we witness the powerful works of God in the world. And
only by your strength and courage do we journey onward as the
People of God. We open our hearts to you now. Come, Holy Spirit,
fill us with your love. We pray through Christ, our Lord. Amen